THE PERSONAL

Mastery

YOUR GUIDE TO SELF DISCOVERY

THE PERSONAL

Mastery

YOUR GUIDE TO SELF DISCOVERY

Kulani Likotsi

THE PERSONAL
Mastery
YOUR GUIDE TO SELF DISCOVERY

First Edition, First Impression 2024

ISBN 978-1-991269-46-1

Website: www.kulanilikotsi.com

Email: info@kulanilikotsi.com

LinkedIn, Instagram, TikTok: @Kulani Likotsi

Published by

FAINOM PUBLISHERS

CONTENTS

FOREWORD i

INTRODUCTION vii

Embracing Vision And Ambition ix

CHAPTER 1:

SELF-IDENTITY (WHO ARE YOU AT YOUR CORE) 1

1. The Key Events That Shaped My Life 8

2. What Do You Choose to Focus On? 23

3. Recognize And Break The Patterns 23

4. Seek Help 23

5. Key Takeaways For You 25

6. Mirror Exercise 26

7. Brand You 29

CHAPTER 2:

SELF-DISCOVERY (WHAT DO YOU WANT) 37

1. Take Time To Review Your Circle Of Influence 45

2. The Importance Of Prioritizing Yourself 49

3. Are You A People-Pleaser? 50

CHAPTER 3:

SELF-LEADERSHIP 65

1. Planning 67

2. Time Management 81

3. Review Your Personal Environment 89

4. Personal Mastery 102

CHAPTER 4:

PERSONAL OWNERSHIP AND ACCOUNTABILITY 109

1. Personal Ownership And Accountability 111

2. Procrastination 120

3. Imposter Syndrome 126

4. Communication 132

CHAPTER 5:

THE JOURNEY TO PERSONAL MASTERY (EMBRACE YOUR PATH) 141

FOREWORD

FOREWORD BY ANTONY HLUNGWANE

In today's fast-paced and ever-changing world, the pursuit of personal mastery has become more crucial than ever. The Personal Mastery addresses a profound need for individuals to deeply understand themselves, align with their purpose, and navigate life's challenges with resilience and clarity. This book emerges as a beacon for those seeking to break free from societal norms, overcome personal limitations, and achieve extraordinary goals.

Many people feel trapped by their circumstances—whether due to societal expectations, personal insecurities, career pressures, or past traumas. The Personal Mastery fills a significant gap by providing a comprehensive guide to self-discovery and personal growth. It empowers readers to challenge the status quo, break generational curses, and create a life of purpose and fulfillment. This is not just a collection of motivational quotes; it is a practical roadmap for anyone determined to transform their life.

The author masterfully captures several key takeaways that promise to leave a lasting impact on the reader. Understanding who you are at your core is the foundation of personal mastery. This book encourages deep self-reflection and provides exercises to help readers identify their values, strengths, and life-changing events. For example, readers might be guided to reflect on significant moments such as the birth of a child or a career change, considering how these events have shaped their identity and perspective.

Readers are also encouraged to articulate their vision and set SMART goals (Specific, Measurable, Achievable, Relevant, Time-bound) to turn their dreams into reality. By emphasizing actionable steps, the book ensures that aspirations are not just fleeting dreams but achievable milestones. For instance, if a reader's goal is to save a million rands within three years, the book breaks this goal into smaller, manageable tasks such as creating a savings plan, investing in property, or starting a side business.

The book also highlights the importance of taking full responsibility for one's actions and decisions. It underscores the benefits of personal accountability, including improved mental health, meaningful relationships, and increased motivation. Practical advice is provided on recognizing and breaking negative patterns, seeking help when needed, and using failure as a stepping stone to greater resilience. For example, it delves into how to overcome common challenges like avoidance or insecurity by seeking professional guidance or adopting new coping strategies.

Moreover, The Personal Mastery offers insights into developing and maintaining a strong personal brand that reflects one's true self, values, and aspirations. Readers are encouraged to remain consistent and authentic in both their personal and professional lives, ensuring that their actions align with their long-term goals. For instance, the book suggests ways to enhance one's online presence to accurately represent their personal brand.

This book is more than a guide; it is a transformative journey. Whether you are a student, a professional, or someone standing at a crossroads in life, The Personal Mastery offers invaluable insights and practical tools to help you unlock your highest potential. It speaks to the dreamers, the ambitious, and those who refuse to settle for mediocrity. By reading this book, you are making an investment in yourself and your future, gaining the knowledge and confidence to turn your vision into reality.

As you embark on this journey of self-discovery and personal mastery, remember that change is constant and growth is a lifelong process. Embrace the lessons, reflect deeply, and take bold steps toward your dreams. This book is your companion—offering guidance, support, and inspiration every step of the way.

May you find the courage to pursue your passions and the wisdom to navigate your path with grace and determination.

Enjoy the journey!

ABOUT ANTONY HLUNGWANE

Antony Hlungwane (CIO-SA) is a distinguished Chartered Chief Information Officer and accomplished Business Executive. Recognized for his visionary leadership, he was awarded the 2024 BPI Foundation Future Leader Award and was a finalist in the IT Web Visionary CIO Awards in 2013 and 2015.

As the founder of Futurecentric Group and CEO of The Unplugg Group, Hlungwane has significantly influenced the business landscape over a career spanning 26 years. He currently serves as the Chairperson of the Board for PROTEC STEM and the Chairperson of the ICT Sub-Committee of the Board for Jet Education Services. Previously, he held prominent roles, including IT Director at MR Price Group and Chief Technology Officer at Hollard.

Hlungwane holds a bachelor's degree with majors in Calculus, Statistics, and Psychology from the University of

Ballarat (Australia), as well as an MBL from the University of South Africa. He is a multifaceted professional: a seasoned business executive, entrepreneur, leadership coach, motivational speaker, lecturer, and researcher.

His passion lies in revitalizing the township economy and empowering local traders to succeed. Through mentoring aspiring IT and business professionals and teaching problem-solving using the design thinking framework, Hlungwane continues to shape the next generation of leaders and innovators.

INTRODUCTION

EMBRACING VISION AND AMBITION

I have encountered a variety of experiences in life that have shaped me into the person I am today. Throughout my journey, there has been much self-reflection, and at times, I've struggled with imposter syndrome, driven by my perfectionist tendencies. I often found myself challenging the norms of the environments around me, always seeking alternative ways to achieve my goals.

Growing up, I became accustomed to constant changes, which taught me to adapt more quickly than many others in my surroundings. From an early age, I learned that nothing is permanent, and the key is to keep moving forward. My exposure to diverse cultures and environments has helped me stay open to endless possibilities. This has been one of the most important lessons of all: change is constant, and the only way to thrive is to keep moving.

Today, I see myself as someone still on a journey of self-discovery, still aligning with my "WHY" and striving for personal mastery. On this journey, I've learned valuable lessons and acquired new skills. I've come to understand that there are many people who share the same vision and ambitious goals I have. That's why I decided to write this guide. If you have a vision and a goal that feels extraordinary, regardless of your background, I want to tell you: yes, it's possible, and you can do it.

We need to be the brave ones who go against the tide, break generational curses, and defy norms. We are the chosen ones, the ones who will not settle for average. We are the ones who will create the change we want to see in our lifetime—and for the generations that follow. I want to give you the validation that your dreams and ambitions are valid. Together, we will turn those dreams into reality, based on how far you are willing to go to make them a reality.

I believe we all have unique talents and gifts that God has granted us. God has a purpose for you, and you need to unleash that purpose. Someone believed in me early on in my journey, and now, as a way of paying it forward, I'm going to share my insights with you. I will also ask you reflection questions to help you on your journey of self-discovery and personal mastery.

There is space for all of us to shine in this multifaceted world. May we each shine in our small corners.

So, I decided to write a book for those who, like me, are sometimes called dreamers and often misunderstood. For those of us who say, "This cannot be it. There must be more to life," or those who say, "I am different from everyone else." This book is your motivation for personal mastery and your guide to use on a day-to-day basis.

Whether you're in corporate, in business, or you're a student—whatever you are, and whoever you are—whatever your big dream and ambition may be, know that I understand how you feel. Together, we will walk this journey. Whatever your background, race, or gender, we are the chosen ones. We are the ones who will build businesses, products, and solutions that no one has ever thought of.

So, enjoy the book and the soul-searching reflection moments you'll have as you master your own personal journey. By the time you finish reading, I guarantee there will be a change in your life. You'll experience a shift in how you operate, how you view yourself, and in how you show up in the world. I'm looking forward to walking this journey with you as we go through the book and get excited about the transformational changes we are about to make.

Enjoy your read!

CHAPTER 1

SELF-IDENTITY (WHO ARE YOU AT YOUR CORE)

We need to start by knowing and understanding who you are. Do you know who you are? Do you know what you stand for? Before we can begin the journey of personal mastery, it's crucial to understand this foundational question. If you don't know what your values are or what your vision for your life looks like, others will fill in those blank spaces for you. So, it all starts with you. What do you truly want?

I know it's a tough question to answer, and this is where personal reflection begins. Who are you? What do you stand for? Do you admire what others have, and think that's what you want too? Are you living according to the plan God has designed for you, or are you constantly looking around, thinking you should be doing what everyone else is doing? The journey begins with this one question: Do you know who you are and what you stand for? Do you know what your values are?

As the first exercise, I encourage you to take some time to write it down. What are your values? What do you believe in? Start here, because everything else will flow from knowing yourself.

Let's begin!

PERSONAL REFLECTION - WHO ARE YOU?

I AM

_____

_____

_____

_____

_____

MY STRENGTHS ARE

_____

_____

_____

_____

_____

I AM PROUD OF MYSELF FOR

_____

_____

_____

_____

_____

MY PURPOSE IN LIFE IS

_____

_____

_____

_____

_____

WHAT I WANT TO CHANGE IN MY LIFE

_____

_____

_____

_____

_____

_____

WHAT ARE THE KEY EVENTS THAT SHAPED
WHO I AM?

_____

_____

_____

_____

_____

We often underestimate the events that have shaped our lives. But the truth is, it's crucial to identify the moments that have changed the way you show up today and how you view the world. It only takes one single event to shift your perspective and shape your character in profound ways.

For example, life-changing events could include:

- The birth of a child

- The death of a loved one (parent, partner, child, etc.)

- A change of location (moving as a family, studying in a new place, working abroad, etc.)

- Graduating from school

- Experiencing loss (job loss, financial hardship, the end of a relationship, health challenges, etc.)

- Freedom (financial freedom, freedom of expression, etc.)

- Acquiring new items (a house, a car, starting a business, etc.)

You'll notice that I've included both the big, life-changing events as well as the smaller moments that have altered your life's course. Both play a significant role in shaping who you are today.

Take some time to reflect on your history and jot down the events that have made an impact. Think about what happened, how it affected you, and how it shaped your perspective.

Now, take a moment and reflect on the key events in your life. Write them down below.

1. THE KEY EVENTS THAT SHAPED MY LIFE

The year and the event description, i.e. on the 13-10-2011 I got married -

Year of Event	Event Description

HOW HAVE THE KEY EVENTS YOU HAVE WRITTEN CONTRIBUTED TO YOUR PERSPECTIVE IN YOUR LIFE?

Situations will arise in your life, but how you respond to them is your choice. While your perspective may be shaped by your current circumstances, how you handle future choices is entirely up to you.

The illustration below stipulates the contributing factors and emotions that get provoked by the events we get to encounter in life and map and shape our current perspective in life – see the below definitions of the below illustration:

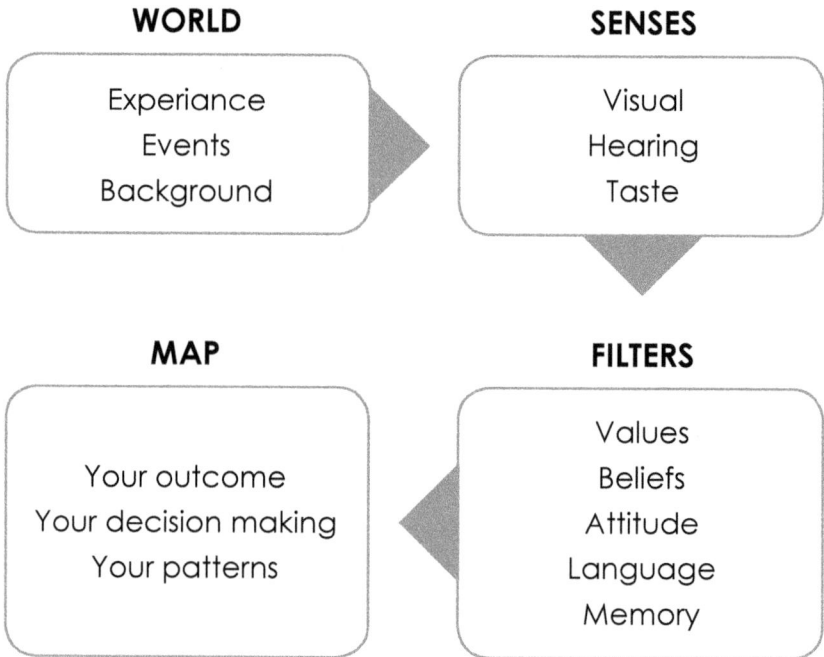

WORLD

Experiance
Events
Background

SENSES

Visual
Hearing
Taste

MAP

Your outcome
Your decision making
Your patterns

FILTERS

Values
Beliefs
Attitude
Language
Memory

1. WORLD

We all perceive the world through the lens of our experiences, backgrounds, and the events that have shaped us. For example, someone who has never been exposed to trauma may see the world as a safe and perfect place, while someone who grew up in a difficult or abusive environment may view the world as a more dangerous or unpredictable place. Both perspectives are valid because they reflect the personal experiences of each individual.

It's important for you to reflect on your own world view. How do you currently see the world around you? For instance, a person who grew up in a high-crime neighbourhood might still remain hyper-aware of potential threats, even if they've since moved to a safer, higher-security area. Despite the change in their environment, their mindset is still shaped by their past experiences.

Awareness of your world view can help you understand how your perceptions are influencing your current life. Are there past experiences that are colouring the way you see things today? If you've endured trauma, you may be seeing the world through a lens that no longer serves you. This can create challenges in areas like relationships, work, or personal growth. For example, if someone has had difficult past relationships, they may struggle to trust others in future relationships because they're carrying the emotional baggage of their past experiences.

Reflection On How You View The World

Take a moment to reflect on the way you view the world.

- Do you see challenges as obstacles or opportunities?

- Are there biases or fears from your past that might influence how you perceive and lead your team?

- How can you re-frame your mindset to foster a more positive, growth-oriented leadership style?

_____

_____

_____

_____

Healing Your World View

Your world view is not static—it's shaped by your mindset and can evolve. Sometimes, healing from past trauma is necessary to allow a new perspective to emerge. Healing is not about erasing your past, but about changing the narrative that you've internalized. The past is what happened, but it doesn't have to define how you see the world today.

For example, when facing challenges, do you focus on the problem or the opportunity? A person who has a trauma-based perspective might be quick to see the problem and become overwhelmed, spiralling into analysis paralysis, asking "Why me?" or adopting a victim mentality. On the other hand, someone who has learned to see challenges as opportunities might immediately start brainstorming solutions or approaches to the problem, seeing it as an opportunity for growth.

Shifting Your Perspective

To create the life you want, it's essential to heal from past experiences that may still be shaping your present world view. Only by shifting to a clearer, more positive perspective can you start to see the world for what it is—a place full of opportunities, not just obstacles.

The world is constantly evolving. The life your grandparents lived is different from the life your parents lived, and the world your children will experience will be even more different. This evolution extends to how we parent, how we work, and how we connect with others. Just as society continues to evolve, your mindset needs to evolve as well. It's crucial to stay open to new perspectives and be clear on how you see the world— so you can embrace the opportunities that await.

2. SENSES

Your world view not only shapes your thoughts but also triggers your senses. The experiences and events you've gone through have left lasting impressions on your body and mind. Your senses—what you see, hear, smell, or even taste—are directly linked to your past experiences.

Think about how certain songs or sounds transport you back to a specific moment in time. Perhaps a familiar song reminds you of a particular event or a time in your life, evoking a flood of memories and emotions. Similarly, the smell of a specific scent can take you back to a moment, like the scent of a loved one's perfume or the smell of food that reminds you of your childhood. Even the taste of particular food can evoke strong memories tied to your past.

Your body creates memories linked to your senses, and these sensory triggers are deeply tied to your world view. Whether these sensory experiences are positive or negative depends on the memories and emotions associated with them. For instance:

- Positive sensory triggers: The smell of a loved one's scent may remind you of cherished moments, making you feel connected, even when they are far away or no longer with you.

- Negative sensory triggers: On the other hand, someone who grew up in a high-crime neighbourhood might feel a rush of anxiety when they hear the sound of an ambulance siren, as it triggers memories of past fear or danger.

- Neutral or nostalgic sensory triggers: The smell of rain on soil might bring a feeling of freedom, reminding you of carefree moments in your youth, when you played in the rain without a care in the world.

These sensory experiences reveal the powerful role that senses play in shaping your world view and emotions.

Reflection On My Senses

Take a moment to reflect on how your own senses—whether sight, sound, taste, or smell—trigger specific memories or emotions. Consider the following prompts:

- What sights (e.g., landscapes, colors, or faces) bring back vivid memories for you?

- What sounds (e.g., music, voices, or environmental noises) transport you to specific moments or feelings?

- What scents (e.g., perfumes, food, or nature smells) trigger emotional responses or connect you to past events?

- What tastes (e.g., favorite childhood meals or foods associated with family) bring back fond or painful memories?

Reflect on how these sensory experiences shape your perspective on the world. Do they bring you closer to your current life, or do they hold you back, tying you to the past?

3. FILTERS

Your background, past experiences, and exposures have significantly influenced your beliefs, values, attitudes, and even how you communicate or remember things. These factors act as filters through which you perceive the world and make decisions. Essentially, how you view and interpret situations today has been shaped by what you've encountered in the past.

For example, think about how your personality and behaviour may have changed due to specific events. Perhaps you've always been a kind and peaceful person until a certain experience or toxic environment caused you to adopt a different attitude. Imagine that you once believed the world was inherently kind, but after encountering people with narcissistic or abusive behaviours, you may have found yourself needing to adopt a more defensive, aggressive stance to survive.

This shift in behaviour shows how an event or experience can drastically alter who you are—transforming a gentle, soft-spoken individual into someone who feels the need to be aggressive to protect themselves.

Your filters are not only formed by events but also by the beliefs and values you were taught. For example, there may be values or principles instilled in you during your

18

childhood that were relevant at the time, but as you mature, you may realize that some of these no longer serve you. They may no longer be applicable or aligned with the person you are becoming.

You are at a place in your life where it's important to filter what you hold onto, and what you let go of. Some principles you were taught will continue to hold true across generations, while others may need to evolve or be refined based on your growth and understanding.

The key is to take ownership of your filters and actively choose what serves you and your well-being.

Reflection On Your Filters

Take a moment to reflect on the filters you currently use in your life. Consider the following:

- What beliefs or values were instilled in you as a child, and how do they influence your current decisions and behavior?

- How have your past experiences shaped the way you respond to situations today? Have you adapted or altered your filters as a result of past events?

- Are there any filters (e.g., negative thought patterns or outdated beliefs) that no longer serve you? What will you do to change them moving forward?

- What principles still hold true for you, and which ones have evolved or need refining to better align with your current journey?

_____

_____

_____

_____

_____

_____

_____

_____

4. MAP

Your world view, the senses that trigger your memories, and the filters you apply to your life shape the decisions you make and reveal patterns in your behavior. Together, these elements provide insight into how you've arrived at the choices you've made up until now.

Yes, your background and past experiences have undeniably shaped your current perspective. However, you hold the power to decide whether you want to continue living according to those past influences, or whether you want to transform and evolve for the better. You can change your world based on how you choose to make decisions moving forward.

By actively choosing to map out your future decisions, you have the ability to create new, positive patterns that lead you toward a more fulfilling and successful life. Your past no longer has to define your future—you have the power to shape your own trajectory.

It's important to remember that you can't control everything that's happened in your past, but you can control your present and future. By taking full ownership of the choices you make today, you can create the life you want and deserve.

Reflection On Mapping Your Future

Take a moment to reflect on your current decision-making patterns:

- How have your past experiences influenced the choices you've made so far in your life?

- Are there any patterns in your decisions that you'd like to change? What new patterns would you like to create moving forward?

- What decisions are you making right now that will map your future in a positive direction?

- What ownership do you need to take of your life to create the trajectory you desire?

_____

_____

_____

_____

_____

2. WHAT DO YOU CHOOSE TO FOCUS ON?

Are you the victim or the victor? Choose one thing that is important to you and focus on it. In order to step into your future positively, you must break free from the negative events of your past. While you can't erase them, you can master the skill of living with them in a healthy, positive way.

3. RECOGNIZE AND BREAK THE PATTERNS

Patterns such as avoidance, the silent treatment, fear mentality, insecurity, seeking reassurance, and attachment are common. Recognize these patterns so you can overcome them. Overcome the victim mentality and seek alternative solutions. Stop generalizing—past events will not produce the same results if you change your thought process.

4. SEEK HELP

Some life events or traumas require professional help. Healing from your past is essential in order to show up as the best version of yourself.

I want to applaud you for taking the time to truly reflect on who you believe you are and what you stand for. It must have been difficult to pause, reflect, and introspect.

REFLECTION

Based on your life key events, identify what events you need to heal from or seek help for. Identify the healing you need and action required to be a better version of self.

_____

_____

_____

_____

_____

_____

_____

5. KEY TAKEAWAYS FOR YOU

1.   Just because you come from a poor background doesn't mean you will remain poor.

2.   Your biases (whether related to gender, race, age, background, social class, etc.) do not define your potential for success.

3.   Shake up your reality and shift your mindset from a victim mentality to one of success.

4.   Review and reconsider the people you surround yourself with, as they influence your life choices.

LOOK AT WHAT YOU'VE WRITTEN AND ASK YOURSELF: ARE YOU TRULY LIVING ACCORDING TO THE PERSON YOU'VE DESCRIBED?

There are two possible answers. Either you're living the life of the person you've written about, or you've described the person you would like to become, not who you are today. I know many of us are not yet living to our fullest potential.

Living as the best version of yourself means aligning with your purest, God-given purpose. If you're still struggling to identify who you are, then this book is for you. Together, we will walk this journey, beginning with the personal reflection you've written about yourself.

Now, think about this: If you were to ask your friends and family who they think you are, do you think their answers would align with what you've written? There's how we think we are, and then there's the reality of how others perceive us.

6. MIRROR EXERCISE

Reach out to at least five people in your life—friends, family, colleagues—and ask them, "Who do you think I am? What do you think I stand for?" Ask them to send you 3 to 5 words that come to mind when they think of you.

Once you've gathered their responses, we'll reflect on these external perspectives and see how they align with your own self-image. Let's begin this exercise and get the mirror reflection of how others see you.

MIRROR EXERCISE RESPONSE

Please write down the responses you received from the five people you reached out to. List the 3 to 5 words they used to describe who they think you are and what you stand for.

This will help you reflect on how others see you and offer valuable insight into your personal image.

Person 1:

Person 2:

Person 3:

Person 4:

Person 5:

MIRROR EXERCISE REFLECTION

Take note of the feedback you received from the people around you. What are the common themes that emerged? Do their reflections align with how you've described yourself? Are there aspects of yourself that they've highlighted which you've never considered before?

Use this time to reflect deeply on who you are and how the world perceives you. Write down your personal insights and thoughts on this exercise.

_____

_____

_____

_____

_____

_____

_____

7. BRAND YOU

Your brand is how the outside world perceives you. It's made up of your values, skills, and experiences, all of which contribute to the public image you project. You need to ensure that the narrative about you is accurate and consistent, no matter where your name is mentioned. Your personal brand can define your reputation—and your reputation is what people see, feel, think, and say about you.

WHAT ARE PEOPLE SAYING ABOUT YOU WHEN YOU'RE NOT AROUND?

What does your name say about you? Your reputation, whether good or bad, is your currency—it determines how you are valued.

As part of building your personal brand, it's crucial to pay attention to what others say about you. This insight will help you identify what changes you need to make to craft the brand you want to be known for. A strong personal brand can attract new opportunities, boost your confidence, elevate your credibility, and build trust with your audience.

People will pay good money for someone with a solid reputation. Those with a strong personal brand are the ones who get the best projects, the most promotions, and are trusted to deliver consistently. They have built a reputation that stands for trust, reliability, and excellence.

You need people to talk about you—especially in rooms you're not in. People invest in those they respect and trust. The more respect you earn, the bigger your network, the better the opportunities, and the higher the rewards.

3 TIPS FOR YOU TO CONSIDER FOR YOU TO STAND OUT

1. **Identify What Makes You Unique.**

    What sets you apart from others? What skills, experiences, or talents do you possess that are rare or hard to find? Recognizing your unique qualities is the first step in building a personal brand that standout.

2. **Define Your Personal Brand.**

    Your personal brand is reflected in how you show up—your appearance, the way you speak, your body language, your network, and your digital presence, especially on social media. Be intentional in crafting an image that aligns with your values and goals.

3. **Maintain a Positive Reputation.**

Reputation is the combination of your uniqueness and your personal brand. It's how people perceive you—what they think, feel, and say about you. Always remember: people are constantly observing you and building a narrative about your character.

Be very clear about the brand you want to build because it directly impacts your credibility. You want to be top of mind when competition arises. How you show up—whether professionally, socially, or personally—should always align with the brand you want to project.

HOW TO SHOW UP AS BRAND YOU

1. **Be Consistent, Authentic, and Intentional.**

Consistency builds trust. If you want people to trust you to deliver on your promises, you must be authentic and intentional in your actions and communications. Trust is the foundation of any strong personal brand.

2. **Refine What Makes You Unique.**

Continuously evaluate and refine what makes you special. Whether it's your skills, knowledge, or product, staying relevant to your audience requires constant attention and evolution.

3. **Be Knowledgeable and Approachable.**

People want to engage with someone who is both informed and easy to connect with. Ensure that every interaction adds value and provides insights to others, building your reputation as someone who can be trusted for both expertise and approachability.

Personal branding can be developed through both in-person engagement (e.g., networking) and online presence (e.g., website or social media). The key is to maintain a consistent and authentic brand across all platforms, ensuring that who you are offline aligns with who you present online:

BE AWARE OF THE FOLLOWING

People often invest heavily in their in-person engagements, putting great effort into how they show up, but tend to neglect their digital presence. It's important to be consistent with your reputation across both. We've all heard of business deals being cancelled because of a single social media comment, as it was seen as a misalignment between someone's in-person brand and their digital brand.

Take a moment to review your online personal brand. Does it align with how you present yourself in person? Remember, your online engagements leave a trail, and how you interact with others online offers a glimpse into who you are at your core and the reputation you uphold.

I hope you now see the common thread that defines you and your offerings. You are constantly selling yourself as a brand—and the way people perceive you will influence their decision to invest in you. People buy into people, and you want them to choose you, promote you, and recommend you. This depends entirely on the strength of "Brand You".

Never stop reviewing how you show up—both online and offline. One way to ensure you're aligned with the brand you want to project is by seeking feedback from others. This will help you understand how you are perceived and allow you to make any adjustments to strengthen your personal brand.

PERSONAL REFLECTION - WHO ARE YOU?

Now that you've written about who you are, received feedback on how others perceive you, and gained a better understanding of your personal brand, do you feel there's anything you'd like to change about yourself? Are there recurring themes that suggest things you need to stop doing or continue doing?

WHAT DO YOU NEED TO STOP DOING?

_____

_____

_____

_____

_____

_____

_____

WHAT DO YOU NEED TO START DOING?

_____

_____

_____

_____

_____

WHAT DO YOU NEED TO CONTINUE DOING?

_____

_____

_____

_____

_____

WHAT IS "BRAND YOU" AND WHAT DO YOU WANT TO BE KNOWN FOR?

CHAPTER 2

SELF-DISCOVERY
(WHAT DO YOU WANT)

1. WHAT DO YOU WANT?

What is your personal vision for your life? What do you want to attract into your world—whether it's something you wish to achieve in the present moment or in the near future? Imagine the possibilities if you weren't afraid or worried about how to reach your ambitions. What if you didn't have to stress over how you would get what you want?

Take a moment to list exactly what you want to attract into your life right now. What feelings are associated with those desires? Do they evoke emotions of excitement, happiness, or anticipation? Notice how your mindset shifts toward positive thinking when you focus on what you want, free from limitations or boundaries.

Now, imagine if you operated from this mindset in all areas of your life—with every ambitious goal and dream in mind. I can guarantee you would feel happier, more excited, and constantly looking forward to achieving your goals.

There's a requirement here for a mindset shift—moving from doubt to living in the possibility that what you want is achievable. A growth mindset involves believing that growth comes from every challenge you face. It means putting in the time, effort, and willingness to learn new skills. The ability to grow allows you to take feedback in a positive way, focusing on how you can improve. When your mindset shifts to one of self-growth, you learn to tune out the negative words and external negativity that may arise.

You must always think about what you want in life with a positive mindset. Whatever you desire should be something that elevates you—emotionally, physically, or spiritually. What are those things you want to achieve? Take the time to write them down or create a vision board.

You need to decide what it is that you truly want, visualize it, and believe that you deserve it. Feel the emotions associated with having achieved your goals.

Never forget to focus on what you're grateful for and to make positive affirmations a regular practice—whether daily or weekly. Repeating these affirmations helps to reinforce your belief in yourself and your ability to achieve everything you desire.

Continuously review your list of desires or your vision board by visualizing it regularly. When you do this, you're creating psychological pathways in your brain that reinforce the possibility of your visions becoming reality. By consistently visualizing your goals, you begin to mentally and emotionally align yourself with the outcome.

Whether you create a vision board or write in your journal, it's important to set goals that are so big they excite and challenge you. As they say, your dreams should be big enough to scare you when you visualize them.

Believe in your vision and truly feel yourself achieving those goals. When you internalize the process and emotions of success, you make it much easier to manifest your dreams.

EXAMPLE OF NAMING YOUR GOAL AND THE BREAKDOWN

Let's say your goal is: "I want to have a million in savings within three years."

1. **Goal (What):**
    Financial goal of saving a million.

2. **When to achieve the goal (When):**
    Within 3 years.

3. **Benefit or Outcome (The So What):**
    Growth in savings and financial security.

4.   The Plan to Achieve (How):

Break the goal down into smaller, achievable tasks.
Examples of tasks could include:
- Investing in property
- Starting or growing a business
- Buying stocks or shares
- Creating a passive income stream
- Saving a set amount each month

By breaking the goal down into clear actions, you create a roadmap that makes the goal feel more attainable. Each small step you take moves you closer to achieving the larger goal.

Now that you've defined your goal, it's time to focus on the possibilities of achieving it. Reflect on the changes you need to make in your life to attract the outcome you desire. What habits, behaviours, or mindsets do you need to adopt in order to reach your goal of saving a million?

Define the actions that will help you achieve your goal. This is where your planning becomes crucial. To be prosperous and live a life of abundance, you must take deliberate action toward smaller tasks and milestones that lead to your larger goal within your 3-year plan.

Set specific targets to be met within a set time period, and regularly track your progress. Monitoring your efforts allows you to stay on course and adjust your approach if necessary.

A goal of saving a million in three years can feel ambitious, but it's achievable depending on your mindset. Start with where you are right now. This is your personal journey and personal goal, so it's crucial to be honest about your starting point.

Yes, you may not have the million right now, but the important question is: What are the actions you need to take today to get there? Do you need to start saving consistently? Do you need to build a business or create a side hustle? Do you need to sell a product or service to generate income?

To achieve this goal, focus and discipline are key. Every small action you take today adds up to larger results over time. Remember, what you focus on, you attract. The more you commit to the process, the more you will draw opportunities, ideas, and resources that move you closer to your goal.

Example, if you constantly focus on negativity, self-doubt, and low self-confidence, there's a strong likelihood you won't reach your goals. When you view yourself from a place of low self-worth or uncertainty, it becomes difficult to attain anything, because you're operating from a low frequency—constantly questioning whether you can succeed.

To achieve anything, you need to change your mindset. Your wealth—in all aspects of life—is rooted in your mindset. Everything starts within your mind. For you to reach your goals, you need to check how flexible and open your mindset is.

We often talk about having a positive mindset and a growth mindset. Both are essential for success. You need to be mindful of what you feed your mind every day, whether it's positive or negative. What you consume mentally shapes how you perceive the world and approach challenges.

Always remember: Your thoughts and feelings manifest into your actions. If you want to change your results, you need to start by changing your mindset and the way you see yourself and the world around you.

While it's important to address self-doubt, self-limiting beliefs, and fear mentality, you need to be cautious not to let these hold you back from taking action. If you are truly committed to achieving your goal of saving a million, it means changing your mindset and possibly the people you surround yourself with.

You need to be intentional about the circle of influence you have. Surround yourself with people who are actively building something—people who are changing their own financial trajectory. The positivity, growth mindset, and planning of those around you will inevitably rub off on you, helping you stay motivated and focused on your own goals.

1. TAKE TIME TO REVIEW YOUR CIRCLE OF INFLUENCE

- Are the people around you motivating you?

- Are they challenging you to push past your limits and reach your goals?

- Or are they reinforcing the same doubts and limiting beliefs that are holding you back?

Review your circle of influence to see if they are motivating or challenging you to reach your goals.

What are you feeding your mindset? What kind of environment are you in, and how is it shaping your thoughts? To achieve your vision, you need to choose to focus on the possibilities rather than the limitations. Have faith that you are going to achieve your goals and believe that you can meet your targets. You must live with the hope that success is inevitable.

Focus on the positive outcome. Even when things don't go as planned, remember failure is feedback. It shows you where you need to adjust, improve, and grow. Failure is simply a lesson—a sign that you need to make changes to move forward at a better trajectory.

One thing I can guarantee you: Even if you experience failure, you are still in a better place than where you started. You're one step closer to achieving your goal than if you had never tried.

Many successful entrepreneurs will tell you they would never partner with someone who hasn't experienced failure. Why? Because failure teaches resilience. Someone who has failed and learned from it is more likely to succeed because they've gained the experience of overcoming challenges and never gave up. They kept pushing until they achieved the outcome they desired.

Use failure as feedback to become better, remember, you become what you think about. If you focus on negativity, you will stay trapped in that mindset and may never achieve the things you truly want. You'll remain stuck in a space of people where growth and progress feel impossible.

Remember:

1.   Don't let fear hold you back.

2.   Don't let your background hold you back.

3.   Don't let other people's failures hold you back.

4.   Use other people's failures as lessons learned in order for you to project yourself going forward.

5.   Don't succumb to the background that you come from.

6.   Focus on what you want.

7.   Don't dim your light by wanting to fit in.

8.   Don't lose sight of the vision you want to achieve.

9.   If you don't have a dream, then you will not achieve much.

CHOOSE YOUR CIRCLE OF INFLUENCE WISELY

In order to achieve your vision, you just need to know that your vision is part of your God-given purpose, and you must hold on to the faith that God will provide what you need to fulfil it. Trust that you will achieve the vision you've been given. Remember: energy flows where attention goes. If you direct your energy towards your vision, it will grow.

So, ask yourself: What are you spending your time and energy on? Are you investing in things that align with your vision? If you truly believe in your vision and can see it clearly in your mind, then you can have it. I stand by this: When you believe in your vision, you will do whatever it takes to make it a reality.

Everything is energy. You have the power to create the world you want to live in. No matter how outrageous or impossible your vision might seem to others, you have the potential to create your own reality.

Your life is yours to create. Follow your excitement. Chase the impossible. Ignore the negativity and doubt from others. You deserve happiness, and everything you've experienced in life has led you to this moment.

No one else has the right to write your story. You are the author of your life, and only you can determine your path.

You are great, regardless of what has happened to you. Your past experiences, no matter how challenging, have brought you to this moment. You don't need to fear your future trajectory. Whatever has happened in your life, whatever struggles you've faced, use those moments to shape the future you want.

Allow yourself to reach your fullest potential but do so on your own terms. Don't let society's standards or the opinions of others define what you can achieve. You have the power to set your own standards and create the life you desire.

Remember, it's always impossible until you begin. Start today. You have everything you need within you to succeed. I trust in your ability—you've got this.

2. THE IMPORTANCE OF PRIORITIZING YOURSELF

I know—it's tough to think about yourself and what you truly want. Often, we become so consumed with helping others and managing everything around us that we forget to take care of ourselves. We lose sight of what we need and what brings us peace.

Have you ever really defined what it is that you want? Do you feel peace in your life? Too often, we focus on pleasing everyone around us, and before we know it, we're caught in a cycle of people-pleasing. We try to ensure everyone else is OK, and in doing so, we forget to take care of ourselves.

As a people-pleaser, you might not even know where to start when it comes to caring for your own needs. You've been so busy taking care of everyone else that setting personal boundaries seems unfamiliar. The truth is, you need to create those boundaries. You need to know when to stop focusing on others' needs and start focusing on your own.

Sometimes, defining what you want is the first step in taking care of yourself. It's a guide to help you navigate your life in a way that prioritizes your well-being. You deserve that peace and balance. It's time to give yourself permission to set boundaries and put yourself first.

3. ARE YOU A PEOPLE-PLEASER?

Here are some trigger questions to help you identify if you're falling into the pattern of people-pleasing:

- Do you find it hard to say no to others?

- Are you constantly apologizing, even when it's not your fault?

- Do you often conceal your feelings to avoid conflict?

- Do you tend to prioritize others' happiness over your own well-being?

- Do you often feel anxious or tense, as if you're walking on eggshells?

If you find yourself answering "yes" to these questions, it may be time to reassess how you're interacting with others—and most importantly, how you're treating yourself.

OVERCOMING PEOPLE-PLEASING

The first step to overcoming people-pleasing is to identify your own needs. It's important to set clear boundaries and be self-aware of who you are and what you want.

EXAMPLE OF IDENTIFYING WHAT YOU WANT

Every time you write or speak about your desires, remember to start with **"I want."** This simple shift in mindset sets your intentions clearly and boldly. Here are examples of what you can focus on:

- I want to be spiritually strong.

- I want to be successful, bold, and courageous.

- I want to fulfil my ambitions, goals, and dreams.

- I want financial freedom.

- I want to be a CEO, a board member, and a trusted advisor.

- I want to be genuinely loved and appreciated.

- I want to be pampered, spoiled, and showered with gifts.

- I want to work hard and play hard.

- I want enough money available to do all my heart's desires.

- I want the soft life.

- I want to be happy, surrounded by love and laughter in my relationships.

- I want to be successful—and to see those around me succeed as well.

- I want generational wealth.

- I want my grandkids and future generations to be prosperous and successful.

- I want my parents to be healthy and live long enough to see my success.

- I want peace, love, wealth, and health.

- I pray that God blesses me so I can be a blessing to others.

- I pray that God hears my prayers, my wants, and needs.

- I pray that God blesses me and those around me, according to His will.

- I pray that God guides my path, blesses all I do, and protects me and my family.

I hope this provides you with a guide to help you clearly articulate what you truly want for your life. Remember, writing down your desires with intention is a powerful step toward manifesting them. Don't be afraid to dream big and claim what you deserve. Your thoughts and words shape your reality—so take the time to write down your aspirations and make them clear, bold, and aligned with your highest self.

You need to start defining what you want. Whether you create a vision board, have your own personal notebook dedicated to your self-discovery, or start journaling your personal journey on this path, you need a place to articulate what you want. So, I ask you to either create a vision board or get your own personal journal now.

Now that you've got that in place, let's begin. What is it that you want to write? Here's the key: when you write in your journal or work on your vision board, you need to be specific about what you want. This journey is all about you. It starts with you. When we ask, "What do you want?" be clear and precise in your answers.

EXAMPLE - PERSONAL FINANCE GOALS

If you have a personal finance goal, here are some considerations to help you define it. What do you want your finances to look like? You need to visualize it. What do you want your take-home income to be? What do you want your business profit margins to look like? Be clear and specific about your financial projections.

What does your investment portfolio look like? How much do you want to settle in debts? Do you want to pay off your credit cards or any other outstanding debts? When it comes to investments and savings, what number are you aiming for? If you're thinking about buying property, what type of property do you want to invest in? If you're planning for multiple streams of income, what is the target amount you want to save or invest?

When we talk about your finances, what are they looking like? These are the types of questions you need to consider as you work toward your financial goals.

Below, write down the personal finances you want to achieve - remember to start your goals with "I want".

MY PERSONAL FINANCE GOALS

_____

_____

_____

_____

_____

_____

Let us now talk about your personal growth. What does that look like? Are you investing in your own personal mastery or personal discovery by getting mentorship and coaching sessions? What do you want to study? What does your personal spiritual growth look like? Do you want to invest in seeking professional help for your past traumas to embark on a journey of personal healing?

Below, write down what you want for your personal growth – remember to start your goals with "I want".

MY PERSONAL GROWTH

At times, we tend to forget about personal grooming. Personal grooming involves learning and practicing the maintenance of personal hygiene and appearance. It can boost your self-confidence and affect how you show up.

How do you want to look? How often do you want to schedule spa treatments? Would you like to regularly book hair, manicure, and pedicure appointments? Define your personal style and the look you want for yourself. What grooming habits do you need to focus on, and how do you want to be perceived? What areas do you need to put more effort into to enhance your appearance? Remember to start your goals with "I want".

MY PERSONAL GROOMING

When we talk about your personal aspirations, what are those? Personal aspirations are your personal goals that can be short-term or future-focused, and they are aligned with your values. Aspirations can fuel your personal drive to live out your purpose.

Example:

- I want to build an app to fix a community gap.

- I want to own my own business.

- I want to open a school.

- I want to start a mentorship program.

- I want to be a director of a company in a specific position or field.

- I want to open an executive coaching program.

What are those personal aspirations that you want to achieve? You want to sit as part of a board of directors. You want to be a board member. What are those things that you aspire to be? Whether you want to have more promotions, more elevations, or more increases. What are those things that you would want to attain as your personal aspirations?

Example: I want to go for media training.

What are those aspirations that will grow you from who you are today into somebody better tomorrow? Remember to start your goals with "I want".

MY PERSONAL ASPIRATIONS

You need to define what your family aspirations look like. What does your family look like? This can be you as a parent, you as a child, you in your parenthood. It talks about how you are as a parent. How approachable are you in your family? How do you prioritize your family life? Your wife, your husband, your kids, your parents. How do you start prioritizing and putting more structure into your family life?

You try to provide for your family, but what type of relationship do you want with your family members? What type of relationship do you want with your kids, your parents? What do you want for your kids as they grow? Do you want kids? How are you making your family members independent? Do you want kids that are well-mannered, bold, intelligent, and humble? What type of family structure and spiritual upbringing do you want? Do you want your kids to be deeply rooted in spirituality?

These are the things you may need to define for yourself when you look at your family. What are some of the family principles you need to have in place? You might also be coming from family traumas, and this means you need to heal first so that you do not replicate those traumas. You need to heal from your upbringing so that you understand what type of family structure you want to create going forward.

You need to heal so that you do not repeat the same cycles and generational curses you come from. You need to create the family structure that you want. You need to be the person who understands that the negative patterns stop with you, and it starts with you to create a positive family structure. You want to have a healthy family structure that future generations can replicate. You want spiritually knowledgeable kids, and you want to teach them prayer.

It all starts with you creating the family structure you desire. Remember to start your goals with "I want".

MY PERSONAL FAMILY

_____

_____

_____

_____

_____

_____

I have given you examples to help guide you in defining what you want. You are now ready to create your vision board or journal your wants. Remember, don't worry about *how* you are going to achieve it just yet; focus only on defining *what* you want. We will address the "how" in the next section.

For now, enjoy the process of creating your vision board or journaling your self-discovery, but before you start, please take a moment to reflect and write down your thoughts below:

REFLECTION

WHAT DO YOU NEED TO STOP DOING?

_____

_____

_____

_____

_____

_____

WHAT DO YOU NEED TO START DOING?

_____

_____

_____

_____

_____

WHAT DO YOU NEED TO CONTINUE DOING?

_____

_____

_____

_____

_____

WHAT HAVE YOU LEARNT ABOUT DEFINING WHAT YOU WANT?

CHAPTER 3

SELF-LEADERSHIP

Self-leadership is about taking full responsibility and ownership of how you pursue and achieve your vision and aspirations. It requires you to:

- Stay true to your commitments and practice self-discipline.

- Continuously engage in self-reflection to foster personal growth.

- Be self-aware and take control of how you present yourself.

- Be mindful of your emotional intelligence and mental well-being, as these factors can impact your ability to achieve your goals.

1. PLANNING

Congratulations on identifying your desires and your vision for your life. This is a significant step in self-reflection, as you have clearly defined your wants, needs, and goals. Now, it's time to take the next step: planning how to achieve your vision. Proper planning involves transforming your ideas and vision into actionable, achievable tasks.

Now that you have identified what it is that you want, what is your vision? You have detailed your wants, needs, and what you want to achieve. Now we move to the next step: planning. You have written down, at a high level, your personal aspirations such as personal finances, personal growth, personal grooming and other personal aspirations.

Define what it is that you want in your life now. You have already identified what you want, but now it's time to figure out how you're going to achieve it. The "How" is crucial because this is where you start breaking down your vision into actionable steps. It is important to have a clear plan—it provides direction and guides you toward your goals.

Always remember, if you do not have a plan, your vision will remain just that—a dream. In order to turn your vision into something implementable, you need to break it down into achievable tasks. Planning also helps with risk mitigation. It forces you to ask the right questions: Do you have the knowledge required? Do you have the right funding? Do you have the right people in place? These considerations are vital to creating a plan that minimizes risks and sets you on the right path.

Let us take the example of building a house. It is not just about wanting a house—it's about planning every detail. You need to know specifics like: What is the size of the house? How man windows will it have? Where will it be located? Is it north-facing or south-facing? What is the surrounding environment like? Is the land secure? These are just some of the key details you need to consider when making your plan.

It is also important to consider innovation in your planning. For instance, if you are building a house for your family, ask yourself if there are new materials or building methods that could help you build more efficiently. Could you use materials that cut down construction time, such as wood instead of concrete? If these alternatives allow you to build faster, how does that affect your budget? These are key factors to consider when planning your project.

Planning also helps you make better decisions. It forces you to prioritize. For example, do you need to build your forever family home right now, or could you start with something smaller that is safe and secure for your family's immediate needs? Is this something you want to achieve now, or is it something you can plan for in the next few years? By creating a timeline, you can better prioritize your goals and focus on what's most important right now.

Prioritization is vital because it helps you decide what to focus on. It allows you to identify what is urgent and what can be accomplished later. For example, building a home is a long-term project, while taking a marketing course for your business might be something you can complete in a month or two. Knowing what requires immediate attention and what can wait will help you stay on track.

In your planning process, do not forget about the people who will help you. You cannot do everything alone. Whether it's building a house or growing a business, you need the right people by your side. Who are the people you need to help you succeed? Do you have the right mentors, coaches, business partners, or stakeholders to assist you? Surrounding yourself with the right people is key to turning your vision into a reality.

As you plan, make sure you optimize your productivity. Not every task needs to be done daily. Some tasks may only need to be completed once a week or once a month. For example, building a house is a large, long-term project that requires more upfront planning, while tasks like improving your marketing strategy could be done consistently but in smaller steps. Knowing how frequently to take action will help you stay focused and organized.

Now that you have your vision, it is time to plan how to achieve it. Let us get started!

To further assist you in your plan on how you are going to achieve your goals and vision, you need to set SMART goals. SMART goals are an acronym that stands for Specific, Measurable, Achievable, Relevant, and Time-bound goals. By setting SMART goals, you ensure that your vision is not just a dream but something actionable, measurable, and achievable. This framework helps you plan effectively and be accountable for meeting your goals.

SMART goals give you a clear roadmap of what you need to do. It is a framework that allows you to create goals that are carefully planned, executable, and trackable. What is the point of having a vision if you don't know when you're going to achieve it? Without a timeframe, your vision remains just a dream—a "one day I'll be this" kind of thought—but you're not taking intentional action toward achieving that goal. You are not putting a plan in place.

So, when you look at your plan, ask yourself: Is it generic, or is it something measurable? Remember, it's always better to take an iterative approach. Break down big goals into smaller, achievable steps. Break the plan into smaller chunks instead of trying to tackle everything at once. That way, each small outcome is attainable, and you can start working on things today that will help you achieve your goal.

PLANNING TO ACHIEVE YOUR GOALS - THE SMART FRAMEWORK

To effectively plan how you're going to achieve your goals, you need to set SMART goals. SMART is an acronym that stands for Specific, Measurable, Achievable, Relevant, and Time-bound. Using the SMART goal framework will help ensure that you plan effectively, stay accountable, and successfully meet your vision. It transforms your big ideas into actionable, trackable tasks.

SMART goals provide you with a clear roadmap of what you aim to achieve. This framework is designed to create goals that are well thought out, executable, and measurable, so you can stay on track and monitor your progress.

Having a vision is essential, but without a plan, your vision may remain just a dream. To avoid living a life full of regrets or missed opportunities, it's crucial to plan and take intentional actions toward achieving your goals. Your plan should:

- Not be generic.
- Be measurable.
- Be attainable.

• Be outcome driven.

Break down your big vision into manageable, bite-sized steps that are practical and achievable. A clear plan gives you direction and helps you move forward with purpose. If you don't have a plan, your vision risks becoming nothing more than a dream.

Let's take the example we discussed earlier about saving a million in three years. Here is how it would look with SMART goals:

• Specific: You want to save a million.

• Measurable: You've set a concrete 1 million—so it's easy to track your   progress.

• Achievable: Yes, it is achievable because you're now looking at the things you need to do to get there: Do you need to buy property and rent it out? Do you need to invest or buy stocks? These are the specific steps you'll take to reach your goal.

• Relevant: Saving a million is relevant to your goal of financial freedom or building wealth.

• Time-bound: You have set a 3-year timeline.

To make it more actionable, break down your plan further. For example, let us say you are saving for property. You can say, "In year one, I need to create a savings account and start putting money in." That is the first tangible step. You are creating a plan with specific, measurable actions.

You could further break it down: In the first six months of year one, you will have already created a savings account and started depositing funds. By the end of the first year, you want to have enough saved to start purchasing property. This approach turns your goal into something manageable and achievable because you have broken it into small, actionable steps.

By making your goals SMART, you make your vision more than just a dream—you give yourself a clear, actionable plan for turning that vision into reality.

REFLECTION

What SMART goals are you going to implement, select 2 key goals you would like to archive and break them down using the SMART framework.

KEY CONSIDERATIONS WHEN PLANNING YOUR VISION

1. Break your vision down into achievable tasks.

2. Identify any skill gaps or knowledge needed for your vision.

3. Determine funding or cost requirements.

4. Identify the people and resources required to achieve your vision.

5. Clarify the duration of your vision (Is it a short-term or long-term goal?).

6. Consider potential risks and how to mitigate them.

Example: Vision: You want to buy a car.

To help you identify how to achieve this vision, consider these questions:

1. What is your affordability budget? (Include monthly repayments, insurance, maintenance, fuel, etc.)

2. What is the purpose of buying the car? (Is it for luxury, or do you need it for practical purposes?)

3. What model of car do you want? (Do you want a brand-new car or a second-hand one?)

4. What type of car suits your needs? (Do you prefer a sedan or an SUV?)

5. How long do you plan to take to pay for the car? (Will you buy it in cash, or will you finance it over 3-5 years?)

By answering these questions, you'll have a clearer plan of how to achieve your goal. Understanding your budget, the type of car you want, and the maintenance requirements will guide you in planning your budget, avoiding financial over-commitment, and choosing the car that fits your vision.

PLANNING FOR INFORMED DECISION-MAKING

Planning empowers you to make better, more informed decisions. It allows you to understand the actions and priorities you need to focus on to achieve your vision. Planning gives you insight into the costs associated with your vision and helps you identify risks and the necessary mitigations.

Using the example of buying a car—whether it's a brand-new car or a second-hand one—requires you to reflect and review your vision based on your current financial situation. Self-discipline is key here: Be honest with yourself about what you can afford, given your financial commitments. For instance, if you can only afford a second-hand car in your current financial state, then it's important to accept that reality. Perhaps, in the future, when your finances are more stable, you could afford a brand-new car. That financial change might come through getting a new job or making a profit in your business. For now, however, buying a second-hand car aligns with your current budget.

THINGS TO CONSIDER WHEN REVIEWING YOUR VISION

1. Time: Do you need what you want now, or can it wait? Is it a short-term or long-term goal?

2. Decision: Is this vision important now, or is it something you can pursue later in life? This helps with prioritizing and making better decisions.

3. Value: Is this vision something that would be nice to have, or is it life-changing? For example, buying a house for your family may be a life-changing

78

decision, while purchasing a sporty car could be a luxury or "nice-to-have" goal.

REFLECTION - MY VISION PLANNING

Looking at your list of personal discoveries and wants, it's time to break those down into achievable tasks. For example, if your vision is to buy a car, follow a structured process like the one below:

Example Vision: I want to buy a car.

Breakdown into Tangible Tasks:

1. Allocate and understand my car budget.

2. Research the option of buying a brand-new car versus a second-hand one.

3. Research different car insurance options.

4. Decide on the repayment method and duration.

This structured breakdown is how you should approach all your visions and goals. Use the space below to select one vision from your list and break it down into actionable tasks as you practice self-leadership planning:

Vision – I want

List actions to take for you to reach your goal

2. TIME MANAGEMENT

As part of your self-leadership journey, it's essential to allocate time for implementing your vision. Setting aside dedicated time to accomplish tasks helps you prioritize and take action. By assigning time to each tangible activity that contributes to your vision, you will be able to meet your goals in a timely manner.

Being intentional about allocating time to achieve your vision will also help you measure:

- Time spent to complete tasks

- Time spent to attain your vision

- Time taken for self-care and personal development

Time management is a powerful tool in preventing procrastination, especially when working towards an ambitious vision. Remember, it's better to miss your self-imposed deadlines than to not start at all due to lack of planning or unrealistic timelines.

You need to be mindful and intentional about where you spend your time. Prioritize your self-development, even when life is filled with competing commitments. There will always be distractions, but this is where you must learn to be selfish with your time. Your actions shape your habits, and your habits define your character. In turn, your character shapes your destiny.

Be deliberate with your life choices, especially regarding how you spend your time, as it reflects what matters most to you. You are responsible for achieving the life you envision. To ensure that life doesn't pass you by while you focus on the wrong things, practice self-discipline by articulating what you want and dedicating time to make it happen. Having a plan of action will help you start living your purpose.

EXAMPLE - BUYING A CAR VISION

Vision: I want to buy a new car.

How: I need to get a new job or be promoted at work to increase my income and afford a new car.

Tangible Actions:	Time Allocation for Each Action:
a. I need to acquire new skills through training to qualify for a promotion.	a. Training to be completed in 1 year.

CHAPTER 3: SELF-LEADERSHIP

b. I need to allocate time for studying and completing assignments.	b. I need to allocate 2 hours during week days and 5 hours on weekends to focus on my school work.
c. I need to apply for the required roles that match my new skills.	c. Daily put in the 30 minutes to search for job adverts that match my skill.
d. I need to find a mentor in my industry to guide me in my career journey.	d. Have monthly mentorship sessions.
e. I need to save money for a deposit on the car.	e. Save 3% of my salary every month for 12 months to accumulate a lump sum for the car deposit.

Reflection: Notice how buying a new car requires multiple activities to be considered (e.g., studying, applying for a job, saving money, and finding a mentor). These tangible actions highlight the necessary steps for making an informed decision about buying a car and provide insight into the time needed to achieve your vision.

You must also make your self-development commitments known to those around you—family, friends, or colleagues—so they understand that your time will now be dedicated to executing your plans, rather than social engagements or other distractions.

In the case of buying a car and going back to school for a promotion, much of your time will be spent on school-related matters, which may impact your social life. Prioritizing time for personal goals can affect relationships, so it's important to maintain a balance.

NOTES ON PERSONAL TIME MANAGEMENT

- Be mindful of your relationships and find a balance between staying true to your purpose and maintaining important connections.

- Avoid overcommitting yourself, which can lead to burnout.

- Steer clear of people-pleasing, as it diverts time away from your own goals by focusing on the needs of others.

- Be intentional with your time—continuously evaluate what you are spending it on and whether it contributes to your goals.

- Review the time you spend on social media and consider how that time could be better used for personal development.

REFLECTION - EVALUATING HOW YOU SPEND YOUR TIME

Take a moment to reflect on the activities that may be consuming your time and preventing you from focusing on your vision. This could be watching too much TV, spending excessive hours on social media, or going out frequently. While it's important to take time for yourself to relax and detox, you need to ask yourself: Are you spending too much time on activities that could otherwise be dedicated to your vision? Remember, we all have the same 24 hours in a day, and it's your personal decision how you choose to spend it.

WHAT DO YOU NEED TO STOP DOING WITH YOUR TIME?

_____

_____

_____

_____

_____

WHAT DO YOU NEED TO DO BETTER WITH YOUR TIME?

_____

_____

_____

_____

_____

Use this space to identify the areas where you can make adjustments. This reflection is about creating more intentionality around your time and how it can better align with the goals and vision you are working towards.

_____

_____

_____

_____

_____

REFLECTION ON TIME ALLOCATION FOR YOUR VISION

Take this time to reflect on the steps needed to bring your vision to life. Below, write down your vision, then list the activities that will help you achieve it. Finally, allocate the time you need for each task. You can either use the vision you've previously articulated or choose a new one.

87

Vision – I want

List actions to take for you to reach your goal:

3. REVIEW YOUR PERSONAL ENVIRONMENT

Your personal environment refers to the spaces and relationships in which you exist. This can include your home life, work environment, and social interactions. Your environment plays a significant role in shaping your reality, influencing your thoughts, actions, and overall behaviour. The values and beliefs you hold may also be challenged or reinforced based on the environment you find yourself in.

Your personal environment can include:

- Your family structure

- Relationship dynamics

- Work environment

- School environment

- Social environment

- Lifestyle choices

HOW YOUR ENVIRONMENT CAN IMPACT YOU

Positive Environment Encourages You to...	Negative Environment Causes You to...
Develop a positive mindset	Stress
Seek growth opportunities	Anxiety
Maintain work-life balance	Depression
Surround yourself with positive-minded people	Panic attacks
Set healthy boundaries	Other medical conditions

You must assess your personal environment and determine whether it aligns with your vision and supports your well-being. This process can be difficult because it requires honest self-reflection on your current environment and its impact on you.

It's important to create a routine that allows you to declutter your mental space and make time for what you truly care about. In today's busy world, personal time may feel like a luxury. Reflect on the past week, month, or even year and ask yourself, "What have I done for *myself*?"

POSITIVE ACTIVITIES FOR A POSITIVE MENTAL ENVIRONMENT

- Exercise

- Journaling

- Reading

- Meditation

- Reviewing your vision

- Setting goals

- Reflection activities

- Going on solo dates

Be intentional about fostering a positive mental environment. Prioritize your time and activities that contribute to your growth. Below is a commitment plan for you to follow:

REFLECTION – PERSONAL COMMITMENT TO CREATING A POSITIVE MENTAL ENVIRONMENT

From today, I will prioritize the following activities to nurture my growth mindset:

You may also consider setting quarterly or yearly commitments as part of your ongoing growth. The key is consistency and discipline in adhering to these commitments.

REFLECTION

_____

_____

_____

_____

_____

_____

Maintaining a positive mental environment will help you in several ways:

- Reduce stress

- Improve coping skills

- Enhance problem-solving abilities

- Promote a healthier lifestyle

- Cultivate better relationships

Remember, this is your life, and you are fully accountable for how you choose to live it.

POSITIVE ENVIRONMENT

A positive environment breeds success, excitement, and optimism. It motivates you to do more and take the necessary steps to achieve your vision. Being in a supportive environment is encouraging because you know there are individuals you can always count on. Surrounding yourself with positive-minded people is contagious; their support can lift you when you're filled with self-doubt. These individuals contribute to your overall well-being and your potential for growth. They walk the journey with you, acting as your trusted, accountable partners. Even when they give constructive feedback, you know their intentions are to help you grow, not to harm you.

CHARACTER TRAITS OF AN ACCOUNTABLE PARTNER

- Offers good advice

- Honest

- Keeps you motivated

- Approachable

- Supportive

- Acts as a sounding board

- Trustworthy

- Provides reinforcement

- Positively challenges you

Take some time to reflect on your accountability partners. Use the traits above as a guide to identify the people who have been your trusted partners throughout your life.

_____

_____

_____

_____

_____

_____

PERSONAL REFLECTION OF YOUR ACCOUNTABLE PARTNERS

_____

_____

_____

_____

_____

I hope you take the time to express gratitude to these individuals who consistently support you. Consider reaching out with a call, a message, or arranging a meeting to openly acknowledge their contribution to your well-being and growth.

When you are in a positive and creative environment, you feel energized. There's a level of excitement to get up each morning and take action toward your vision.

NEGATIVE OR TOXIC ENVIRONMENT

On the other hand, a negative or toxic environment can have the opposite effect. You may feel anxious, depressed, or even experience panic attacks. There is no room for growth in a toxic environment. If you find yourself in an environment that forces you to change your authentic self, act in a way that's against your values, or behave negatively, it's essential to find ways to remove yourself before it further harms you.

If you're constantly in internal conflict, unable to align with your true self, it's crucial to make a decision about your next steps. When you recognize that your environment is contributing to mental health issues or other health conditions, I urge you to seek medical and professional help. Your well-being is paramount.

Society or financial pressures may compel you to stay in a negative environment, but ultimately, the decision to prioritize yourself is yours. This is a big decision, and I encourage you to seek support as you navigate the necessary changes.

REFLECTION ON MY NEGATIVE PERSONAL ENVIRONMENT

Take time to reflect on your current environment and identify any negative activities or influences that need to change. These could include:

- People-pleasing

- Emotional, mental, physical, or spiritual abuse in your relationships (family or friends)

- Toxic work environments. The first step in addressing these issues is acknowledging areas in your environment that are not serving you or your vision. This awareness is essential to making progress toward your goals.

MY NEGATIVE PERSONAL ENVIRONMENT IS

_____

_____

_____

_____

_____

THE DECISION I AM MAKING

_____

_____

_____

_____

_____

THE ACTION I AM TAKING

_____

_____

_____

_____

_____

It's not easy to admit that changes are needed, especially when those changes involve altering parts of your life that no longer align with your vision or purpose. But the journey toward your desired life starts with you. Only you have the power to change your environment.

KEY CONSIDERATIONS FOR REVIEWING YOUR PERSONAL ENVIRONMENT

- Understand your environment.

- Focus on what you can control.

- Be honest with yourself about the vision you have for your life.

- Define and plan the environment that best supports your goals.

- Articulate both the positive and negative elements of your environment.

- Be bold and courageous in making decisions that serve your vision.

- Adjust your environment to align with your goals.

- Seek help when needed (mentally, physically, emotionally, spiritually).

Some decisions may be more difficult, so be sure to seek support as you continue on your journey.

OVERALL REFLECTION - HOW DO YOU FEEL ABOUT REVIEWING YOUR ENVIRONMENT?

Now that you've reflected on your environment, consider how you feel. Is your environment positive or negative? What have you discovered about yourself? What are your key takeaways, and how will you show up differently moving forward?

_____

_____

_____

_____

_____

_____

_____

YOU ARE PERSONALLY ACCOUNTABLE FOR

- Your life and its outcomes.

- What you want to achieve.

- Reaching your goals and fulfilling your dreams.

- How you show up, day after day.

You are responsible for the direction of your life. You cannot blame others for how your life turns out.

TRAITS OF SOMEONE WHO PLAYS THE BLAME GAME

- Blames their background or upbringing.

- Blames external factors (e.g., the government, others).

- Struggles to take personal accountability for their life choices.

Stop making excuses and blaming others. The difference between someone who has mastered personal accountability and someone who hasn't is that the accountable person takes full ownership of their actions, including their mistakes, knowing there are consequences for their choices.

Taking responsibility for your actions, both positive and negative, requires honesty with yourself. When making decisions to achieve your vision, you must be prepared for both success and failure and treat failure as an opportunity to learn.

4. PERSONAL MASTERY

Personal mastery is the process of understanding how your words, thoughts, and actions align with your vision, purpose, and belief system. It is a continuous journey of self-improvement and seeing life from a broader perspective. Personal mastery isn't a one-time goal, but rather an ongoing commitment to living in alignment with your purpose and living a fulfilling life.

PRINCIPLES OF PERSONAL MASTERY

- Be self-aware: Understand who you are, your strengths, weaknesses, and what drives you.

- Be authentic: Show up as your true self.

- Be clear on your vision: Understand your life's purpose and direction.

- Embrace continuous learning: Adopt a growth mindset and be open to learning from your experiences.

- Be resilient: Bounce back from challenges and setbacks.

- Be disciplined: Stay committed to your goals and responsibilities.

- Be emotionally intelligent: Regulate your emotions, especially during stressful or challenging times.

Personal mastery requires you to live in alignment with your values. Your values define what you believe is good or bad, right or wrong. For example, values such as courage, honesty, compassion, and integrity shape how you navigate life. Personal mastery may require difficult decisions, like sacrificing something in the present to achieve something greater in the future.

TRAITS OF PEOPLE WITH HIGH PERSONAL MASTERY

*   Driven and purpose-focused.

*   Self-aware, constantly evaluating their reality and making necessary changes.

*   Positive outlook on life.

*   Change-makers who challenge the status quo.

*   Community builders, always connecting and supporting others.

You have the potential to reach a high level of personal mastery. The choice is yours to make how you show up and how you take personal accountability for your life. Every day, you must consciously decide to remain true to your purpose and not be consumed by your environment.

WAYS TO DEVELOP PERSONAL MASTERY

- Establish a morning routine: A consistent morning routine can set the tone for your day and help you approach it with clarity and focus.

- Practice gratitude: A mindset of gratitude fosters positivity and sets the right tone for your day.

- Avoid self-sabotage: When things go wrong, don't internalize blame. Learn from mistakes, but don't let them define you.

- Manage your emotions: Build emotional intelligence by recognizing and regulating your emotions, which helps you respond more effectively to others.

- Explore different paths: Try new activities, hobbies, or career paths to discover what resonates with you.

- Seek inspiration: Read books, listen to podcasts, or attend workshops to gain fresh perspectives and insights.

- Set specific goals: Align your goals with your values and long-term aspirations.

- Embrace challenges: View setbacks as opportunities for growth, learning, and development.

PERSONAL MASTERY - A CELEBRATION OF YOU

Personal mastery is about continuously growing, learning, and showing up as the best version of yourself. It's not just about achieving big goals, but also celebrating the small wins along the way, learning from mistakes, and using those experiences to become better every day.

CELEBRATE YOURSELF

- Celebrate your small wins: Every step forward is progress, no matter how small. Take pride in your achievements and acknowledge the effort it took to reach them.

- Learn from your mistakes: Mistakes are not failures; they are opportunities for growth. Use them as feedback to do things better next time.

PERSONAL TAKEAWAY NUGGETS

- Every accomplishment starts with the decision to try - You can't reach your goals if you don't take that first step. The decision to start is the first victory.

- Set your vision and work hard to achieve your goals - Clarity of vision will guide your actions. Once you have a clear vision, commit to working towards it every day.

- Rise above the noise - The world is filled with distractions, opinions, and negativity. Stay focused on your goals and don't let the noise pull you off course.

- Celebrate your wins, no matter how small - Whether it's a big achievement or a small one, take the time to celebrate your progress. These small victories add up to bigger ones over time.

- Build networks (mentors, coaches, sponsors) - Surround yourself with people who believe in your potential, challenge you, and offer guidance along the way. These relationships are crucial to your growth and success.

NOW, TAKE ACTION

Look at what you've written down. Read it aloud to yourself and feel the power of your vision. Then, get up and take that first step. Do what needs to be done, even if it's just a small action. Do this every day, every week, and every month, and before you know it, you will be right where you envisioned.

REFLECTION

Now that you have read the book and understand what Personal Mastery is. What are you going to do, to show up differently from today going forward? What is your personal commitment towards your personal mastery and self-discovery?

_____

_____

_____

_____

_____

CHAPTER 4

PERSONAL OWNERSHIP AND ACCOUNTABILITY

1. PERSONAL OWNERSHIP AND ACCOUNTABILITY

Personal Accountability is your understanding and ownership of the consequences resulting from your behaviours, actions, and the choices you have made in life. It's about taking responsibility for how you show up in every aspect of your life.

How you show up contributes to your personal branding. What are you known for? The way you present yourself can reflect your personal accountability. When people look at you, what do they see? How you show up can portray someone who is trustworthy, dependable, and willing to take ownership of everything they do. You become someone who stands up for opportunities because you are accountable and driven by what you want in life.

It is essential to take full ownership of your present self, acknowledging the past experiences that shaped you but choosing to remain optimistic about the future. When you take positive personal accountability for your life, others may see you as a leader. Your actions and mindset can inspire others to work with you or partner with you, which goes back to how you are perceived. Be mindful of the impression you leave on others by showing that you are responsible for your actions and goals.

Your life journey is a personal discovery and a process of mastering your own path. You are responsible for your actions and the life you live. Personal ownership means taking full responsibility for the decisions you make and how you show up in the world. Personal accountability involves understanding and accepting the consequences of your behaviours, actions, and choices.

Be mindful that, as you take personal accountability for your dreams and goals, others may be watching. They might see a leader in you. They might recognize someone they are willing to work with or partner with. This ties back to your personal branding and how people perceive you. Your actions and behaviours give others the perception of how responsible you are and how capable you are of taking charge.

You are personally accountable for your life. You are personally accountable for what you want in your life. You are personally accountable for achieving what you need and for making your dreams a reality. You cannot blame anyone else for how your life turns out. That's the difference between someone who has mastered personal accountability and someone who plays the blame game.

When you take full ownership of your actions, you understand that there are consequences—both positive and negative. On the other hand, someone who blames their background, upbringing, or government, and constantly looks outside themselves, misses the point. They don't ask, "What have I done about the life that I want!"

Taking responsibility for your actions requires honesty with yourself. When you make personal decisions and work to make your vision a reality, you need to stop making excuses and blaming others.

BENEFITS OF PERSONAL ACCOUNTABILITY AND OWNERSHIP

- A Change in Mindset: You will develop a growth mindset. You'll recognize setbacks, but you'll also take responsibility for transforming those failures into positive outcomes. This is where growth happens.

- Improved Mental Health: When you take full ownership of your responses to everything around you, your mental state improves. Personal accountability allows you to manage challenges with a positive outlook, which directly impacts your overall well-being.

- Meaningful Relationships: Accountability in how you show up in your relationships builds trust and respect. You'll notice your relationships will improve because your actions align with your values, and you take responsibility for the role you play in them.

- Increased Motivation: When you realize that your success or failure is on you, you become more driven. The moment you stop doing things for others and start doing them for yourself, your motivation skyrockets.

You are motivated to perform because it's your personal dream, your ambition, your vision that you want to drive. And isn't that better? Knowing that you are living your best life, doing your utmost to achieve your personal goals?

One of the key benefits of personal accountability is that you start learning from your mistakes. It's about understanding that yes, you will fail at certain tasks, and yes, you will make mistakes but the beauty of it all is that you get to learn from them. You get to pick up the lessons that will propel you to do better next time. When you take ownership and accountability for your life, greater benefits come your way.

TIPS TO HELP YOU WITH PERSONAL ACCOUNTABILITY AND OWNERSHIP

1. Be Clear About Your Responsibilities: When you define what it is that you want to achieve and how you are going to achieve it, you need to hold yourself accountable. Be very clear about the role you play and the responsibilities you have so you understand what is expected of you. You need to model that responsibility and be honest with yourself, even when you make mistakes. If you've done wrong, apologize and take steps to correct the situation.

2. Take Action: Writing things down is not enough. There is a continuous requirement for action. You need to constantly review the actions required and track your progress. You can't just sit and wait for things to happen; you need to actively put in the work. Learn from your mistakes, consider them as learning opportunities, and apply those lessons moving forward.

3. Learn from Failures: Learning from failures is not just about your own experiences. It is also about observing others. If someone else has failed in a similar endeavour, ask yourself, what did they do wrong? By learning from others' mistakes, you

can avoid repeating them and propel yourself to achieve things faster and better. Do not replicate the mistakes of others. Instead, extract the key learnings so you can improve and move forward more effectively.

4. Find a Mentor or Coach: It is essential to find someone who can hold you accountable and help you stay on track. A mentor or coach can provide invaluable guidance, offer feedback, and help you stay focused on your goals. They have already travelled the road you're walking, and their experience can help you navigate the challenges ahead. Mentors and coaches help you identify blind spots, direct you when you lose your way, and keep you aligned with your vision.

5. Seek Feedback: Feedback is a powerful tool for self-awareness. It helps you understand how you are showing up and highlights areas where you might be falling short. Feedback can be both positive and constructive, and it is important to be open to it. Sometimes feedback can be brutal, but you need to assess whether it is being given in a constructive way—whether it's meant to guide you or pull you down. You need to be able to filter the feedback that you get, and this is where those mentors and coaches will also help and guide

you. Sometimes, you need to ignore the noise and focus on the true essence of the feedback you're receiving. Are there individuals who might struggle to give you information or feedback in a manner that you can consume? If so, ignore the noise and find the silver lining. Focus on the true essence of the feedback they're giving you.

REFLECTION: PERSONAL OWNERSHIP AND ACCOUNTABILITY

What are your thoughts on your own personal ownership and accountability? How can you commit to being more accountable in your life? Consider the following questions:

- What will you stop doing?

- What will you start doing?

- What will you continue doing?

I will Stop:

I will Start:

I will Continue:

REFLECTION

2. PROCRASTINATION

Procrastination is the act of intentionally delaying action on your responsibilities or goals. It's when you find ways to postpone pursuing your purpose, which often leads to feelings of guilt, anxiety, lack of motivation, and even stress.

UNMASKING PROCRASTINATION: 4 WAYS IT SHOWS UP

• Avoidance – This is when you avoid putting in the effort required to achieve your goal because it feels difficult or overwhelming. The complexity of the task can leave you feeling paralyzed or unsure where to start. To overcome this, it's important to build sufficient motivation and interest in achieving your goals. Take personal pride and ownership in the life you want to create. Remember, it's your choice to do the hard, complex tasks that will enable your dream to take shape. Break down your larger goal into smaller, manageable steps to make it less daunting. By procrastinating or avoiding these necessary tasks, you risk increasing your stress, guilt, and anxiety, as you delay the progress toward your goal.

- "I Don't Have Time" – This is when you keep yourself busy with everything except your goal, leading to poor time management. To avoid this, minimize distractions that take away from the time you've set aside to work on your goals. You are responsible for meeting your own deadlines and objectives. Common distractions include social media, social gatherings, lack of planning, and poor prioritization. If you don't take accountability for planning your time effectively, it will lead to missed deadlines, reduced productivity, and a failure to achieve your desired outcome. You don't want to find yourself rushing to complete something that doesn't meet your personal standards or the quality you aim for.

- Being a Perfectionist – You may feel the need for everything to be perfect before you can consider your goal complete. However, not everything will meet your ideal standard. To help manage this, apply the 80/20 rule—focus on achieving 80% of the desired outcome, knowing that the remaining 20% can always be refined later. What you have at the moment is enough. Be self-aware and recognize when you're holding onto a task or goal that could already progress in its current state. Seek guidance and feedback from your accountability partners or mentors, who can offer insights and help you move forward.

- Fear of Failure – You may delay pursuing your goal because you fear failing. It's important to remember that failure always carries valuable lessons that can help you improve and do better next time. Start training your mindset to see unknown situations as opportunities for learning, rather than fearing potential failure. The key is not to let fear stop you from living your dreams; instead, use that fear to fuel positive action and the execution of your goals. No matter how much you fear failure, keep moving forward and take action anyway. The worst that can happen is that you learn from your failure, and you'll be better off for having tried your best and gained valuable lessons along the way. On the other hand, not starting due to fear only keeps you stuck.

- Fear of failure can negatively impact your health, leading to depression, anxiety, panic attacks, and low self-esteem. Be sure to stay self-aware and seek professional help if needed.

OVERCOMING PROCRASTINATION

You can overcome procrastination, but it's a journey that requires you to take full ownership and accountability for meeting your goals. It starts with believing in yourself and your ability to turn your dreams into reality. Be kind and patient with yourself along the way. This can be achieved by implementing the following steps:

1. Be clear on what you want to achieve.

2. Break your goal into manageable tasks (create a to-do list to avoid feeling overwhelmed).

3. Improve time management by scheduling all your activities and commitments.

4. Track your progress and celebrate every win—big or small.

5. Find an accountability partner or mentor who will keep you honest, track progress, and encourage self-reflection.

Remember the SMART framework we discussed earlier. This tool can help you overcome procrastination and plan your goals more effectively. SMART stands for Specific, Measurable, Achievable, Relevant, and Time-bound goals.

Finally, take the time to reflect on what you're procrastinating on and how you can begin to overcome it. The first step is awareness and action.

PROCRASTINATION REFLECTION

Take a moment to reflect on what you're currently procrastinating on. Are you avoiding tasks because they feel difficult? Do you feel like you don't have enough time? Are you caught up in perfectionism, or are you fearing failure?

REFLECTION

Reflect on the strategies you will use to tackle procrastination. What steps will you take to break free from avoidance, time management struggles, perfectionism, or fear of failure?

_____

_____

_____

_____

_____

_____

_____

_____

_____

3. IMPOSTER SYNDROME

As you strive to achieve your goals, it's common to experience self-doubt, especially when you're taking on challenging tasks. You may question whether you're capable or worthy of success—this is what's known as imposter syndrome.

Imposter syndrome occurs when you doubt your own skills and talents. It's the uncomfortable feeling of believing you're incompetent or undeserving of your achievements. This can lead to anxiety, insecurity, and emotional or mental distress. Remember, imposter syndrome often arises from being overly self-critical.

This feeling of self-doubt can resemble anxiety, where you constantly feel that you're not enough or that you don't deserve to reach your goals. This insecurity can also contribute to procrastination, as you hesitate to move forward due to fear of not measuring up.

Even with countless personal achievements, imposter syndrome can make you feel unworthy or lack confidence in your abilities. Almost everyone experiences this phase, especially when they're tackling ambitious goals or stepping outside their comfort zone. So, don't worry if you find yourself dealing with imposter syndrome. Instead of letting the doubt paralyze you, use it as fuel to build your self-confidence and prove to yourself that you are capable.

Celebrate your progress and achievements, rather than allowing self-doubt and limiting beliefs to overshadow your success.

SYMPTOMS OF IMPOSTER SYNDROME

1. Self-Doubt – You question your ability to achieve your goals and doubt your competence, even when evidence shows you're capable.

2. Self-Undermining – You downplay your worth by avoiding contributions, believing you're incompetent or not deserving of success.

3. Self-Deflecting – You shy away from praise and recognition, deflecting credit by attributing success to external factors rather than acknowledging your own role.

4. Self-Sabotaging – You avoid success to prevent setting higher expectations for yourself, subconsciously undermining your own potential.

5. Self-Burnout – You push yourself excessively to prove your worth, trying to overcome feelings of incompetence, which can lead to exhaustion and emotional strain.

6. Perfectionism – You feel the need to overperform or be flawless in order to overcome feelings of inadequacy and prove that you're capable.

SIX COMMON IMPOSTER SYNDROME TRAITS

1. Over-Preparation – You tend to over-prepare or overthink, fearing that you're not fully ready or competent.

2. Difficulty Seeking or Receiving Help – You hesitate to ask for help or accept support, believing it shows weakness or incompetence.

3. Struggling with Feedback – You find it hard to accept feedback, often interpreting it as criticism rather than constructive guidance.

4. Negative Self-Talk – You frequently engage in negative self-talk, doubting your abilities and focusing on your perceived flaws.

5. Difficulty Celebrating Success – You downplay or even dismiss your achievements, feeling undeserving of recognition.

6. Perfectionism – You feel the need to be flawless in order to prove your worth or competence, leading to excessive pressure on yourself.

Imposter syndrome can stem from various factors, including your environment, background, personality type, or specific character traits. While these feelings may cause anxiety, it's essential to focus on cultivating a positive mindset. Don't let imposter syndrome stop you from pursuing your goals.

YOU CAN OVERCOME IMPOSTER SYNDROME

Overcoming imposter syndrome is a continuous journey of self-discovery and personal accountability. It's a choice you make every day to confront self-doubt and take action to close the gap between where you are and where you want to be. With persistence, self-compassion, and support, you can break free from the grip of imposter syndrome.

Here's a refined version of your Tips to Overcome Imposter Syndrome and Imposter Syndrome Reflection, with improvements in clarity and flow:

Tips To Overcome Imposter Syndrome

1. Practice Positive Self-Talk – Use positive affirmations and avoid negative self-sabotage. Remind yourself of your worth and capabilities regularly.

2. Cultivate a Growth Mindset – See mistakes as opportunities for learning. Embrace challenges and focus on upskilling in areas where you feel less confident.

3. Celebrate Your Wins – Whether big or small, take time to celebrate your achievements. Recognize your progress and honour your efforts.

4. View Feedback as a Gift – Learn to receive feedback with an open mind. Use it as a tool to grow and improve, rather than seeing it as criticism.

5. Seek Support – Don't hesitate to reach out for help. Whether it's from a medical professional, therapist, mentor, coach, or a trusted friend, support is key. You can also invest in self-help books, podcasts, or courses to deepen your personal growth.

IMPOSTER SYNDROME REFLECTION

Reflect on your own experiences with imposter syndrome. What traits of imposter syndrome do you recognize in yourself? What specific actions will you take to overcome them? You can use the list of traits above as a reference.

Be self-aware of your self-doubt and take ownership of your journey. Craft a development plan to address these feelings, and commit to building your confidence and self-assurance. The more proactive you are in your approach, the more control you'll have over your personal growth.

My imposter syndrome trait	How I will overcome (Development plan)

REMEMBER, WITH IMPOSTER SYNDROME, BE PATIENT AND KIND TO YOURSELF

It's important to be patient and compassionate with yourself as you work through imposter syndrome. Pace yourself according to the goals you've set, and recognize that you are deserving of all the blessings and success you've achieved—and the success yet to come. You've worked hard to reach where you are, and that effort deserves recognition. Never stop working toward your growth and purpose.

Focus on your personal journey, and avoid letting self-doubt hold you back. Run your own race at your own pace, because no one shares the same dreams, ambitions, or path that you do.

4. COMMUNICATION

Effective communication is essential as you embark on your personal mastery journey. You will make lifestyle changes and personal decisions that may challenge the status quo, and at times, you may find yourself distancing from others to focus on your goals and purpose. During this process, it's important to recognize that there are people in your life who may need to be included in your journey.

As you evolve and mature in your personal growth, you'll experience changes that will need to be communicated effectively to those around you— whether it's family, friends, colleagues, your partner, mentors, or medical professionals.

Tips for Communicating Your Personal Mastery Journey

1.   Clearly Express Your Commitments

Communicate your intentions, goals, commitments, availability, and the resources you need. Let the people in your life know your plans and how they can support you, so they understand your focus and priorities.

2.   Be Authentic When Facing Challenges

When you're facing personal frustrations, it's important to be authentic in your communication. Let those around you know if you're struggling so that your actions and non-verbal cues aren't misinterpreted. This helps avoid negative impacts on your relationships.

3.   Apologize When Necessary

Understand that your personal mastery journey won't be perfect; you will make mistakes. When you do, take full accountability and apologize. A simple "sorry" can go a long way in mending relationships and fostering growth.

4. Practice Active Listening

Listening is just as important as speaking. Whether receiving feedback from mentors or hearing perspectives from family members, practice active listening to absorb information clearly. Seek to understand where others are coming from and appreciate their viewpoints.

5. Remember Communication is a Two-Way Process

Communication isn't just about speaking your truth; it's about listening as well. Be mindful of the balance between speaking and listening. Self-awareness of how you communicate and how you listen will enhance the effectiveness of your interactions.

COMMUNICATION PLAN

The tips provided above are just examples, and you may find alternative ways to effectively communicate your goals to others. Now that you have a clearer idea of how to communicate, it's important to create a communication plan tailored to your needs and journey. A communication plan involves outlining the key aspects of how and when you'll communicate your goals, commitments, and progress. This ensures that you're intentional and organized in how you engage with those who are part of your journey.

Key Elements Of A Communication Plan

1.   What You Want to Communicate

Clearly define what you need to share—this could include your goals, commitments, intentions, and the purpose behind your actions.

2.   When You Want to Communicate

Decide on the frequency of communication: will it be weekly, monthly, quarterly, or annually? Determine the best intervals based on the nature of your goals and relationships.

3.   Who You Want to Communicate With

Identify the key people you need to involve in your journey—family, friends, colleagues, mentors, therapists, etc. Tailor your communication to each group's role and influence on your progress.

4. **How You Want To Communicate**

Choose the method of communication: will you communicate verbally, through written updates, or a combination of both? Consider the preference and effectiveness of each method for your audience.

5. **Where You Want to Communicate**

Identify the platforms or environments where communication will take place: online, phone calls, or in person. Choose the medium that fosters the best connection and clarity.

COMMUNICATION REFLECTION

Below is an example of how you can apply the communication tips and communication plan to effectively share your intentions and the impact of your actions with those around you. To guide your reflections, I've included prompts in parentheses under each heading to help you think through your responses.

Goals And Communication Plan - Example

Goal	What (What you want to communicate)	Communication Plan (When, Where, How)	People to Engage (Who)
I want to go to school	Communicate my intention to go back to school and limit my time on social gatherings to focus on personal development.	In-person meetings or phone calls with key people to inform.	Family and friends
I want a new job	Share my goal of securing a new job and the steps I plan to take to achieve it.	Monthly online sessions for 6 months to get guidance on job search strategies.	Mentor or coach

REFLECTING ON YOUR GOALS AND TASKS

Take a moment to reflect on the goals and tasks you've defined for yourself throughout this journey. Revisit all the commitments and intentions you have set, and consider how well you've been communicating these to yourself and those around you.

Goal	What (What you want to communicate)	Communication Plan (When, Where, How)	People to Engage (Who)

UNDERSTANDING YOUR PERSONAL JOURNEY

It's important to recognize that your purpose is not a community project; it is your own personalized journey. Along the way, you will often be misunderstood because of the ambition and drive you have. Not everyone will grasp the depth of your vision or understand the path you're on.

Mastering the skill of effective communication is essential, but it's equally important to know how much you share about your goals. Be prepared for the fact that not everyone will understand your journey, and that's okay. It's a part of the process.

Embrace being misunderstood, undermined, and even disregarded at times as you walk the path of self-discovery. These moments can be challenging, but they are also opportunities for growth and resilience.

By taking ownership and accountability in how you communicate your journey, you create a space for others to understand your purpose and ambitions. This can, in turn, inspire those who resonate with your path to join you as allies or partners in your journey of personal growth.

CHAPTER 5

THE JOURNEY TO PERSONAL MASTERY (EMBRACE YOUR PATH)

Personal mastery is a lifelong journey of continuous self-refinement, self-improvement, self-development, and reflection. Be patient with yourself and your journey, as we all have different purposes in life. While we may start our paths together, it doesn't mean we will achieve the same things at the same time. Your vision, purpose, and goals are uniquely yours, not determined by your family, friends, or the environment around you.

Stay true to who you are and what you want in life. Your self-identity should align with who you are and what you do. Be mindful of your desires and never allow life's pressures to cause you to lose your identity. Remember, you are your own brand, and it is essential to uphold the "Brand You" to your own high standards.

Never stop learning or seeking growth. Don't let the environment dictate who you should be. Continually seek opportunities for self-development while holding yourself accountable to fulfil your vision and purpose. Life will inevitably present obstacles and challenges, but you have the power to choose to overcome them and rise above the noise to fulfil your God-given purpose. Never lose sight of what you want in life. You are responsible for your actions, so take full ownership of how you conduct yourself on your journey.

The reflections you've explored throughout this book are just the beginning of your lifelong journey of personal mastery and self-reflection. I hope you've been genuine and honest in this process. Understand that it's not a one-time exercise but a continual journey of self-refinement. Throughout the book, you may have uncovered traumas that require healing, and I encourage you to seek professional help for your emotional and mental well-being. Healing will only contribute positively to who you are and may even break generational cycles of trauma.

By adopting some of the principles shared in this book, you have already taken significant steps toward personal mastery.

Here are some final insights for your self-discovery journey:

- It starts with you and the choices you make.

- Celebrate yourself.

- Celebrate your wins, no matter how small.

- Learn from your mistakes and use them as feedback to do things better.

- Every accomplishment begins with the decision to try—so don't stop trying.

- Set your vision and work hard to achieve your goals.

- Rise above the noise.

- Your self-growth will often happen in isolation; it is not a community project.

- Be intentional about where you spend your time.

- Build networks of support (accountability partners, mentors, coaches, sponsors, etc.).

Review all your reflections, read them out loud, and make a personal decision to plan and take action. Make this a regular practice (daily, weekly, or monthly), and before you know it, you will be living within your purpose and vision.

May God reveal to you your true purpose. May you remain steadfast in living out that purpose. May you lead a life full of fulfilment and direction. May you never lose hope in who you are meant to be. Allow yourself to embark on this journey of self-discovery and finding your purpose. Never stop imagining the life you want for yourself. Be the dreamer with a clear plan to achieve your vision and goals.

www.ingramcontent.com/pod-product-compliance
Lightning Source LLC
Chambersburg PA
CBHW070444090426
42735CB00012B/2453